Also by Joe Lasker
MOTHERS CAN DO ANYTHING
NICK JOINS IN

HE'S MY BROTHER

Story and Illustrations by
JOE LASKER

Albert Whitman & Company
Morton Grove, Illinois

To my children, David, Laura, and Evan

Library of Congress Cataloging-in-Publication Data

Lasker, Joe
  He's my brother.
  SUMMARY: A young boy describes the school and home
experiences of his younger brother who has a learning disability.
  1. Home and school—Juvenile literature. 2. Slow learning children-
Juvenile literature. [1. Mentally handicapped.] I. Title.
HQ773.7.L35   301.42'7   73-7318
ISBN 0-8075-3218-5

Text and Illustrations © 1974 by Joe Lasker.
Published in 1974 by Albert Whitman & Company,
6340 Oakton Street, Morton Grove, Illinois 60053.
Published simultaneously in Canada by
General Publishing, Limited, Toronto.
All rights reserved. No part of this book may be reproduced or transmitted
in any form or by any means, electronic or mechanical, including
photocopying, recording, or by any information storage and retrieval
system, without permission in writing from the publisher.
Printed in the United States of America.
15   14   13   12   11   10

Jamie's my brother.
He doesn't have many friends.

Little kids play with him.

Sometimes a big kid plays
when no one else is around.

Jamie gets teased.
He doesn't know how to answer back.

When he tries, he gets in trouble,
and comes home.

Becka is our sister.
She likes Jamie.
She bakes brownies for him.

When kids on the block choose up teams,
they choose Jamie last.

It took Jamie a long time

to learn to tie his shoelaces.

He still has trouble
hanging up his clothes.

I guess I have, too.

School is easy for me.
But hard for Jamie.

Jamie gets mixed up at school.
Especially when it gets noisy.

When it's time for a test,
Jamie thinks he knows the answers.
Then everything goes wrong.

Sometimes the kids make fun of Jamie.

They take his cookies
or spill his milk.

Sometimes I get mad at him
because he is so slow.

Then I feel sorry and play
a game of checkers with him.

But there are things Jamie likes a lot.
He loves babies.

He loves animals.
He never hurts them.

One day Jamie said,
"Wouldn't it be nice
if we could be friends
with all the animals in the world?"
I wish I'd thought of that!

Sometimes Jamie gets mad.
He comes home,
and he slams the door.
He says, "I hate school!"

Mom says, "Oh, Jamie.
You had a bad day."

Jamie goes in his room.
He plays his drums loud!

He's a good drummer.
All the kids say that.
He plays boom,
boom-boom, BOOM!
He feels better.

At school, teacher says
Jamie doesn't know he's doing it,

but he is always beating out a rhythm,
over and over.

Jamie likes to draw, too.
Once he drew two hundred
fire trucks.
He really did.

He does things over and over.

Mom helps Jamie with his schoolwork.

Dad reads to Jamie.

I make up stories for Jamie.
Stories to tell him we love him.

He laughs.
He's my brother.

The Invisible Handicap

Jamie suffers from 'the invisible handicap.' Children like him cannot be pigeonholed. They are not retarded.

But their uneven growth and development confuse them and lead others to unrealistic expectations.

These children may look 'different.'

They may be physically clumsy.

They may have difficulty in making judgments, especially in social situations.

They may have unusual difficulties with one or more of the three R's.

They suffer feelings of inadequacy and poor self-image.

We hope this book will enable other Jamies and their families to identify with the experiences shown and take comfort.

Mildred *and* Joe Lasker